Coloring Book for Adult

This coloring book belongs to

_ _ _ _ _ _ _ _ _ _ _

Merry
CHRISTMAS

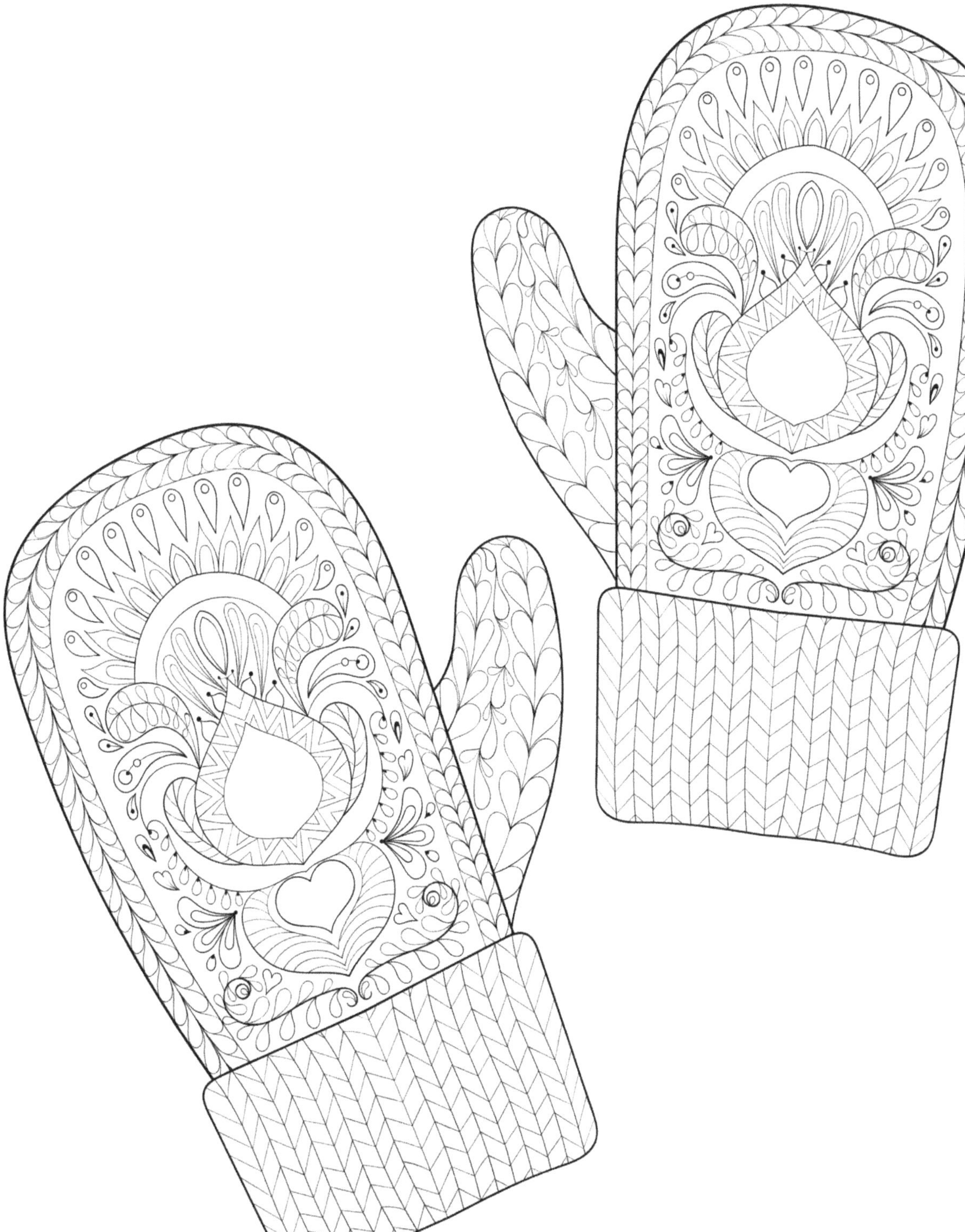

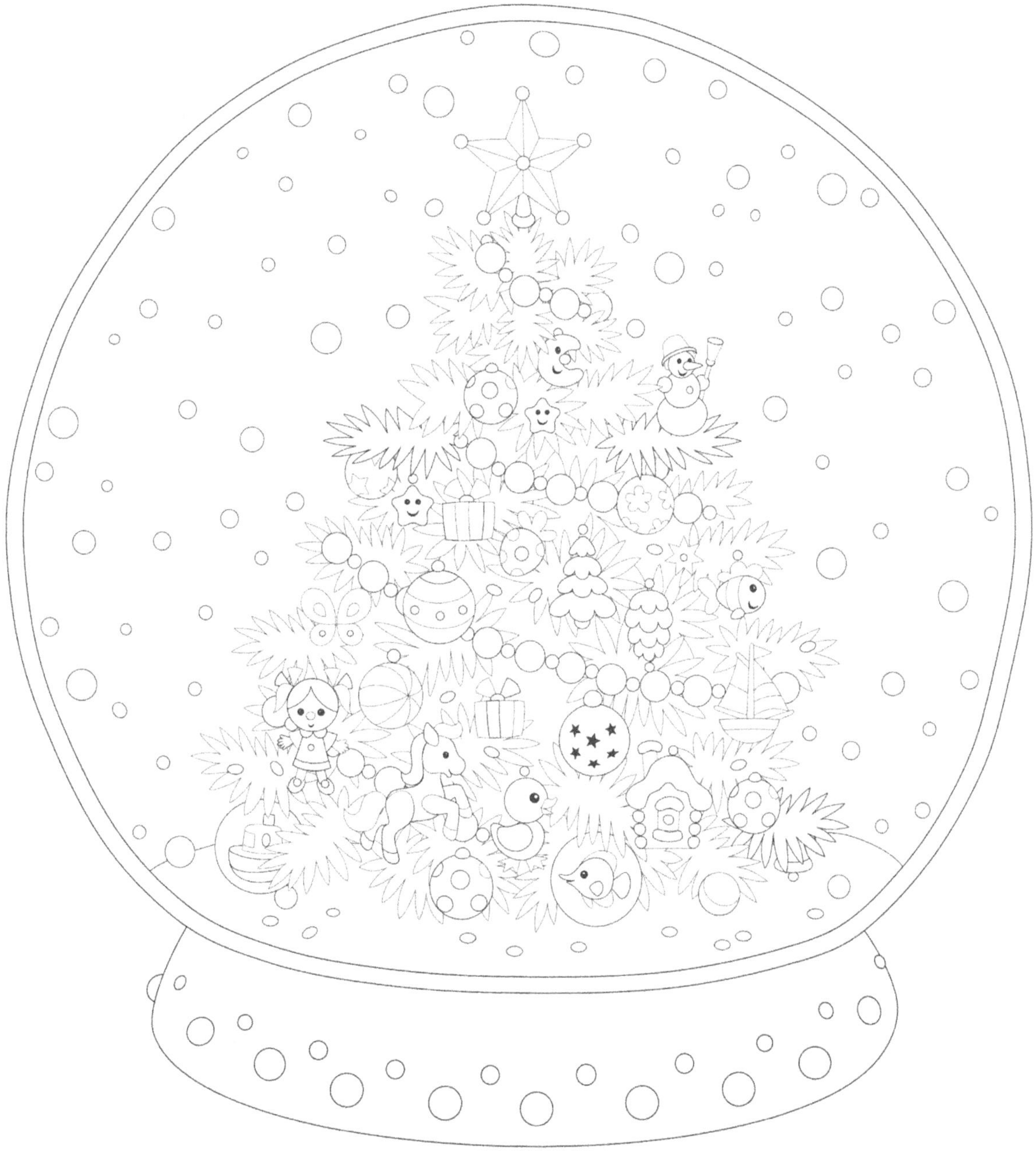

MERRY
CHRISTMAS!

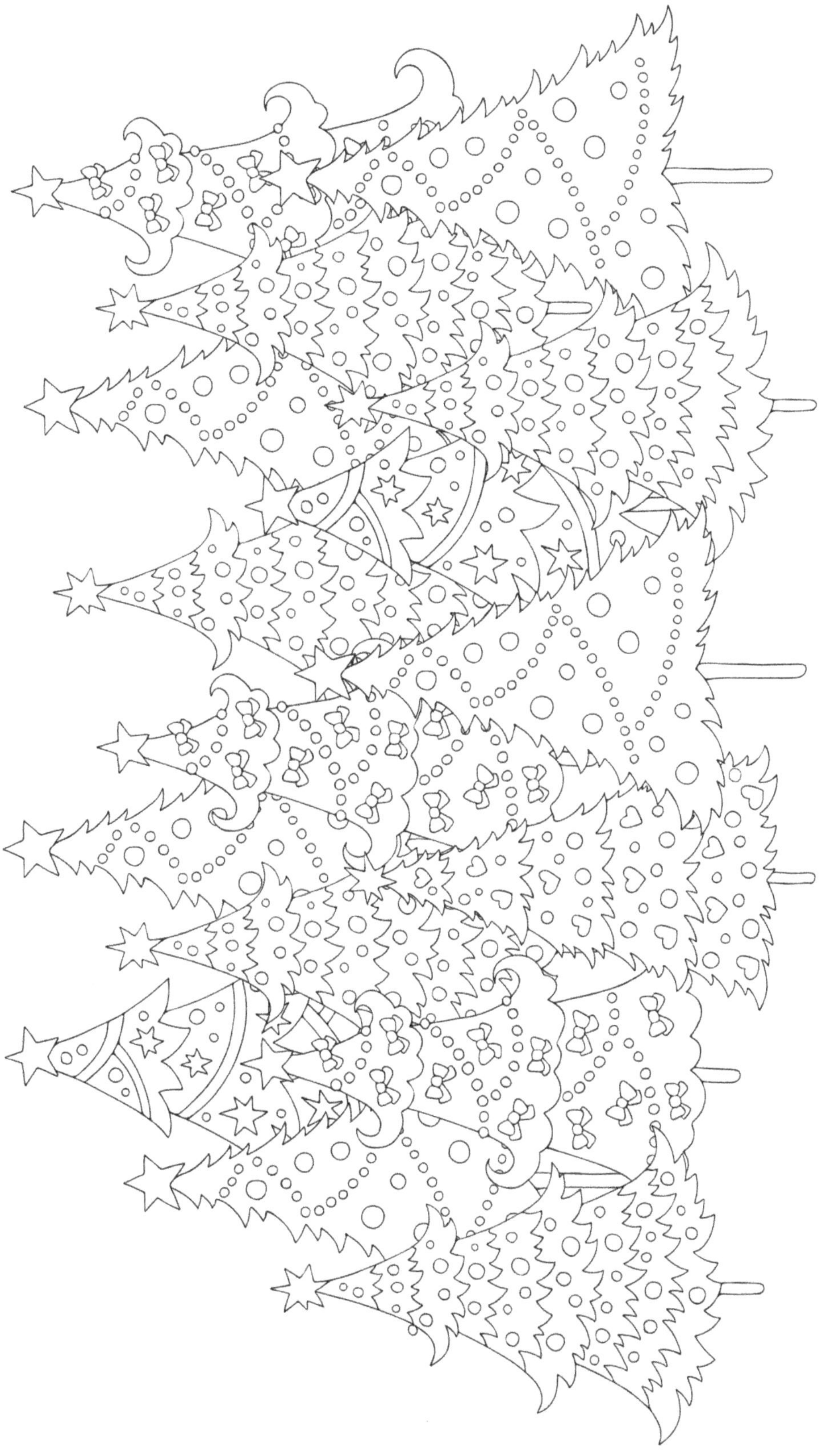

www.ingramcontent.com/pod-product-compliance
Lightning Source LLC
Chambersburg PA
CBHW082158171224
19196CB00013B/839

9 798554 979668